PAPER PLANES

PAPER PLANES

This edition published in 2013 by Arcturus Publishing Limited
26/27 Bickels Yard, 151–153 Bermondsey Street,
London SE1 3HA

ISBN: 978-1-78212-289-0
CH003655EN
Supplier 13, Date 0813, Print Run 2543

Models and photography: Michael Wiles and Belinda Webster
Text: Jenni Hairsine
Design: Grant Kempster and Tokiko Morishima
Edited: Annabel Stones and Samantha Noonan

Printed in China

Contents

Welcome

...to the high-flying world of making paper planes!

In this book, you will discover how to create the most incredible aircraft. From sleek jets to jumbo gliders, you can have a huge fleet of your own, all made from paper!

Before you begin, you need to know which way up your paper is.

Portrait
means this way:

Landscape
means this way:

You can make the planes in this book with any rectangular piece of paper. Thinner paper works better.

Jets

Jets are all about speed!

These super-speedy favourites are sleek and simple to make, but they're stable, strong and fun to fly! They can be anything you want them to be, from Boeing 747s to fighter planes like Raptor or Falcon.

The Original

The original – and some might say best – paper plane design!

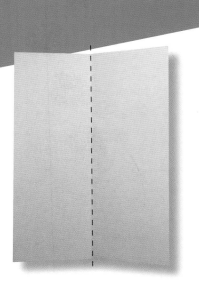

1 Place your paper so that it is portrait. Fold it from left to right down the centre line, then unfold it again.

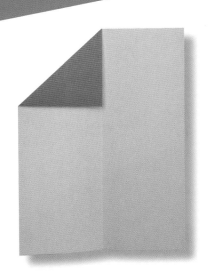

2 Fold the left-hand corner into the centre, making sure to line up the top edge with the centre crease.

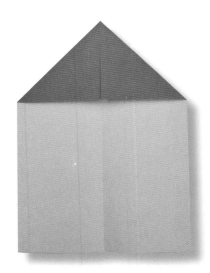

3 Repeat step 2 on the right-hand corner.

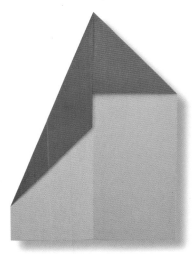

4 Fold the top left-hand diagonal side into the centre crease.

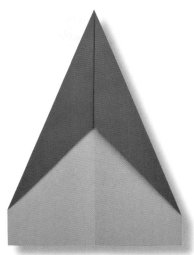

5 Repeat step 4 on the right-hand diagonal side. Your jet plane is taking shape!

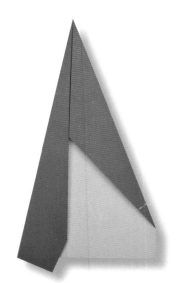

6 Now carefully fold the left-hand diagonal side again into the centre crease.

7 Repeat step 6 on the right-hand diagonal side. You need to press the folds harder as the paper gets thicker.

8 Turn over your jet plane, keeping the point at the top.

9 Fold the right side over to the left, using the centre fold you made in step 1.

10 At the bottom of your plane, lift the top flap a little bit and fold a small triangle. Then unfold it so that it is slightly raised.

11 Turn over your plane and repeat step 10.

12 Now your jet plane is ready for take-off! Carefully open out its wings, aim high and watch it fly.

The Classic

A classic jet with added aerodynamic features.

1 Place your paper so that it is portrait. Fold it from left to right down the centre line, then unfold it again.

2 Fold the left-hand corner into the centre, making sure to line up the top edge with the centre crease.

3 Repeat step 2 on the right-hand corner.

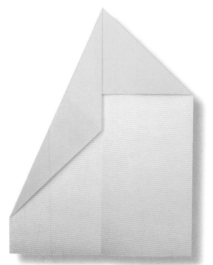

4 Fold the top left-hand diagonal side into the centre crease.

5 Repeat this step for the right-hand diagonal side.

6 Fold the left side over to the right, using the centre fold you made in step 1.

7 Lift the top flap and fold it over to the left. It should overlap the straight edge a little bit, as shown. This forms the first wing.

8 Turn your plane over and repeat step 7 to form the second wing. Make sure the wings are the same size.

9 Now fold back the top wing a little to create a wing tip.

10 Turn over your plane and repeat step 9 for the second wing, making sure the folded edges align with each other.

11 Holding the plane by the long centre fold, open out the wings and adjust the wing tips – you're ready to fly!

Dashing Dart

An aerodynamic flat plane
with piercing performance.

1 Place your paper so that it is
landscape and fold it down
the centre from left to right.
Now unfold it again.

2 Fold the left-hand edge
into the centre, lining up
the left edge with the
centre crease.

3 Repeat step 2 on the
right-hand side of the
paper, so that the two
outside edges now meet
at the centre crease.

4 Now fold down the top
left-hand edge so that
it aligns with the
centre crease.

5 Repeat step 4 on the top
right-hand edge, so that a
point is formed at the top.

6 Fold the top left-hand
diagonal edge into the
centre, aligning with
the centre crease.

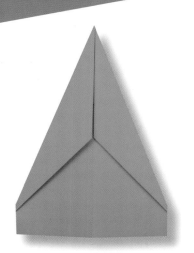

7 Repeat step 6 on the top right-hand diagonal edge.

8 Now fold the new left-hand diagonal edge into the centre, again aligning with the centre crease.

9 Repeat step 8 on the right-hand side. You will need to press more firmly as the folds make the paper more resistant.

10 Turn the paper over so that the wings are underneath.

11 Fold the right-hand side over to the left, using the centre fold you made in step 1. Make sure that the edges align and are not overlapping.

12 Holding all the central folds together, open out the wings to form a flat surface on top of the plane. Your dart is ready to dash through the sky!

Speedy Spear

You'll need absolute precision to make this thin, javelin-like spear.

1 Place your paper so that it is portrait. Fold it from left to right down the centre line, then unfold it again.

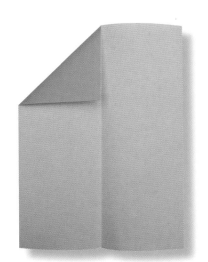

2 Fold the left-hand corner into the centre, making sure to line up the top edge with the centre crease.

3 Repeat step 2 on the top right-hand corner and align at the centre crease. Open out the folds.

4 Fold the top left-hand corner down into the first diagonal fold line.

5 Repeat step 4 on the right-hand side.

6 Now carefully fold the left-hand corner towards the centre crease, using the crease you made in step 2.

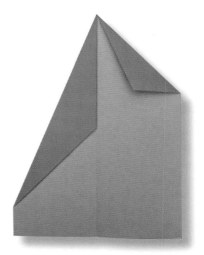

7 Repeat step 6 on the right-hand corner.

8 Now fold the left-hand edge of the paper in towards the centre crease again.

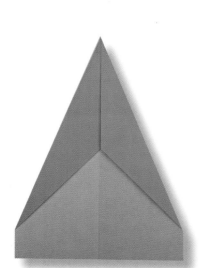

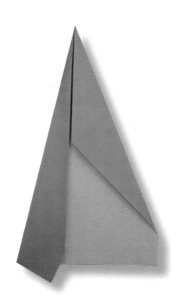

9 Repeat step 8 on the right-hand side.

10 Fold the long left-hand edge of the paper in again towards the centre crease. As the paper gets thicker you'll need to press more firmly.

11 Repeat step 10 on the right-hand side, making sure the edges align along the original centre crease.

12

Repeat this fold one last time, beginning with the left-hand side, making sure the outside edge aligns with the centre crease and the tip is a precise point.

13

Repeat step 12 on the right-hand side.

14

Turn the plane over so the folds are underneath and then fold it in half from left to right, using the centre fold you made in step 1.

15

Fold the top flap over to the right, starting halfway down the edge of the plane, as shown.

16

Turn the plane over and repeat step 15 on the other side. Make sure that these new flaps align.

17

Hold the plane by the centre fold, open out the wings and adjust the edges. Your speedy spear is ready to throw!

Sky Warrior

Sky Warrior's stealth-like qualities make this speedy jet so impressive.

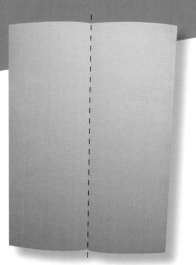

1 Place your paper so that it is portrait. Fold it from left to right down the centre line, then unfold it again.

2 Fold the top left-hand corner diagonally so that the top edge of the paper aligns with the right-hand edge. Unfold it again.

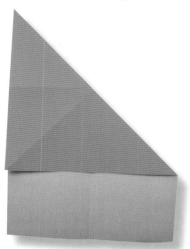

3 Repeat step 2 with the top right-hand corner and then unfold the paper.

4 You will now have a cross with a central point. Turn your paper over.

5 Fold the top of the paper down, making sure your fold goes through the centre of the cross. Unfold the paper and turn it over.

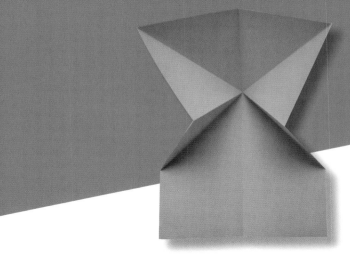

From underneath, carefully push up along the horizontal fold lines and press them inwards so they meet in the centre. Press down on the cross folds left and right.

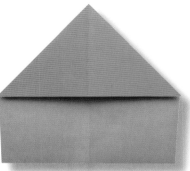

7 Press the top edge down so that you form a triangle shape at the top.

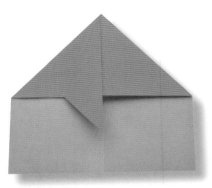

8 Fold down the top left flap of the triangle into the centre crease, as shown.

9 Repeat step 8 on the right-hand side to form a diamond shape in the centre of your paper.

10 Now fold the left-hand side of your diamond into the centre crease. Press firmly as the paper becomes more resistant.

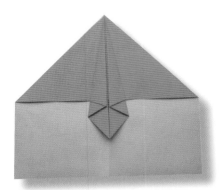

11 Repeat step 10 on the right-hand side of the diamond.

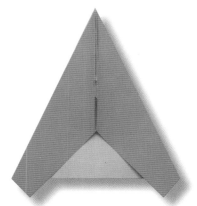

12 Lift both edges of the diamond so they form an elevated section in the centre. You'll need to keep this raised while you make the next folds.

13 Now fold the left-hand side of the plane into the centre crease.

14 Repeat step 13 on the right-hand side of the paper.

15 Once again, fold the left side into the centre crease.

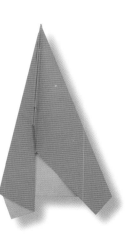

16 Repeat step 15 on the right-hand side of the paper.

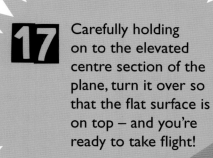

17 Carefully holding on to the elevated centre section of the plane, turn it over so that the flat surface is on top – and you're ready to take flight!

The Javelin

The Javelin is the perfect paper plane to fly long distances.

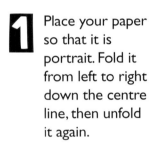

1 Place your paper so that it is portrait. Fold it from left to right down the centre line, then unfold it again.

2 Fold the left-hand edge of the paper into the centre crease.

3 Repeat step 2 with the right-hand edge of the paper, making sure both edges align along the centre crease.

4 Fold the top left-hand corner down so that it aligns with the centre crease.

5 Repeat step 4 on the right-hand corner. You will have a triangle shape at the top of your paper.

6 Fold the top left-hand diagonal edge inwards to align with the centre crease.

7 Repeat step 6 on the right-hand diagonal edge, making sure both edges align at the centre crease.

8 Turn your paper over and fold it in half, from right to left, using the centre crease you made in step 1.

9

Lift up the right-hand corner of the top flap and fold it diagonally from just below the nose almost to the bottom left-hand corner.

10

Turn your plane over and repeat step 9 on the left-hand corner.

11

Take the bottom flap and fold it up in the same way as you did in steps 9 and 10. Now, unfold it.

12

Turn the plane over and repeat step 11 on the other side, using the crease you just made.

13

Open out your plane, as shown. You will see a 'W' shape. From underneath, push the bottom part of the centre crease upwards and pinch it together.

14 Press the plane together, so the tail fin is pointing upwards inside, and press down on all the folds.

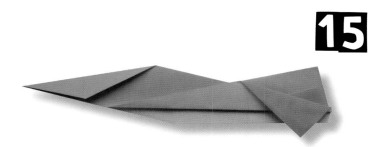

15 Now fold the top point downwards so it aligns with the back of the plane.

16 Turn the plane over and do the same on the other side.

17 You open out the nose and tail flaps and your brilliant javelin is ready to fly!

Excel-R8

As its name suggests, the
Excel-R8 jet is the one to beat!

1 Place your paper so
that it is portrait. Fold
it from left to right
down the centre line,
then unfold it again.

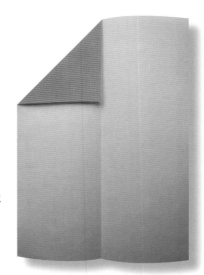

2 Now fold the top
left-hand corner
downwards, so that
in aligns with the
centre crease.

3 Repeat step 2 on the
right-hand corner.

4 Fold the top central
point downwards so
that it is a short way
from the bottom
edge, as shown.

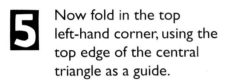

5 Now fold in the top left-hand corner, using the top edge of the central triangle as a guide.

6 Repeat step 5 on the right-hand corner.

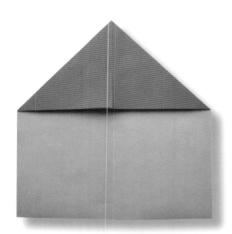

7 Now fold your big triangle back upwards. Use the bottom straight edge of the small triangles as the guide for where to fold.

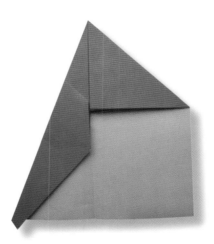

8 Fold the left-hand side into the centre, making sure that the diagonal edge aligns with the centre crease.

9 Repeat step 8 on the right-hand side.

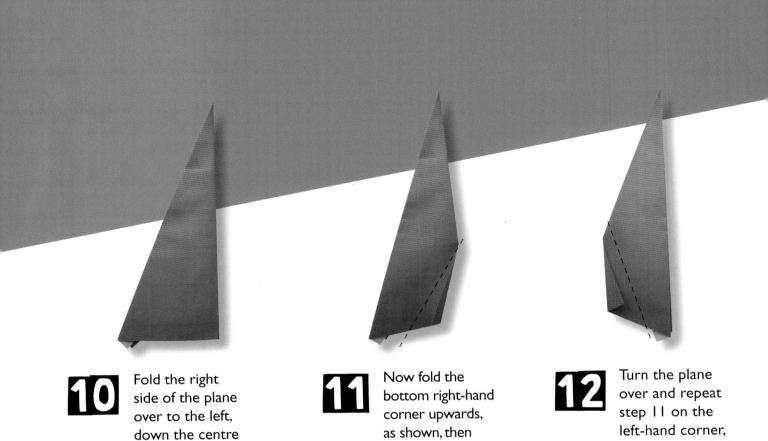

10 Fold the right side of the plane over to the left, down the centre fold that you made in step 1.

11 Now fold the bottom right-hand corner upwards, as shown, then unfold.

12 Turn the plane over and repeat step 11 on the left-hand corner, reversing the fold you just made.

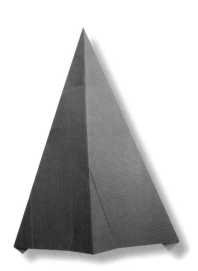

13

Now turn the plane so that the coloured side is facing up and the nose is pointing away from you. The folds you made in steps 11 and 12 will have created a small triangle that meets at the centre fold. Push this inwards as you fold the plane at the centre fold.

14 Holding the plane so the side is facing you, press firmly on the folds you have just made. Now fold one top corner down horizontally to form the wing. The fold should be parallel to the bottom edge of the plane.

15 Turn the plane over and repeat step 14 to create the other wing, making sure they align with each other.

16

Your truly excellent jet plane is ready to 'Excel-R8' through the air!

Gliders

Gliders are the cruisers of the paper plane world!

Stable and elegant, the gliders' large wingspan makes them perfect for slow, long-distance flights. So what are you waiting for – get folding, get outside and get gliding!

Nakamura

Get ready for a folding frenzy with the Nakamura, with its clever extra fold.

1 Place your paper so that it is portrait. Fold it from left to right down the centre line, then unfold it again.

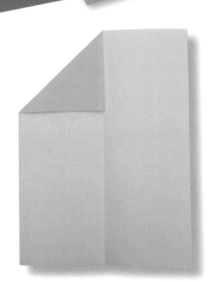

2 Fold the left-hand corner into the centre, aligning the top edge with the centre crease.

3 Repeat step 2 on the right-hand corner.

4 Fold down the top point, making the crease along the horizontal line created by your previous folds.

5 Now fold the point of your triangle back upwards a short way, as shown. Make a crease and unfold.

6 Fold the top left-hand corner towards the centre crease. They should meet half way between the top edge and the bottom point of the triangle.

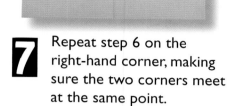

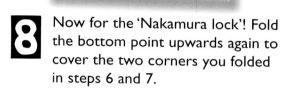

7 Repeat step 6 on the right-hand corner, making sure the two corners meet at the same point.

8 Now for the 'Nakamura lock'! Fold the bottom point upwards again to cover the two corners you folded in steps 6 and 7.

9 Turn the plane over and fold it in half from left to right down the centre crease that you created in step 1.

10 Now fold the top flap to the left to create a wing. Your fold should run parallel to the straight edge.

11 Turn the plane over and repeat step 10 to create the other wing. Make sure the two wings are the same width.

12 Open out the wings to form an aerodynamic surface and your Nakamura glider is complete!

33

The Spade

Dig deep into your paper-folding repertoire to create this ultra-cool Spade.

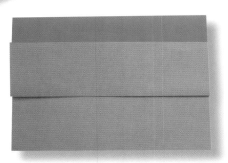

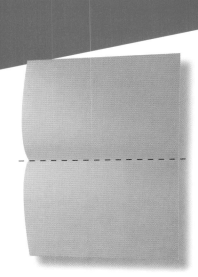

1 Place your paper so that it is portrait, then fold it in half, along the centre from top to bottom.

2 Now fold the bottom edge of the top sheet back up towards the folded top edge. Stop a little way from the edge, as shown.

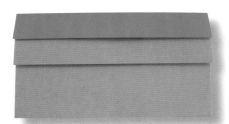

3 Now fold down the top edge so that it goes over the edge you have just folded upwards.

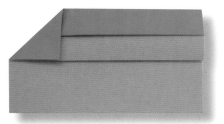

4 Fold the top left-hand corner towards the centre so the left-hand edge aligns with the bottom fold.

5 Repeat step 4 for the right-hand corner. Press firmly on the creases.

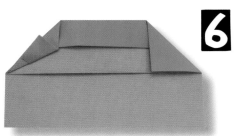

6 Now fold the bottom point of the left-hand triangle towards the top edge and make a crease. Start the fold from the left-hand edge where the horizontal fold is. Unfold it and then fold it in the other direction, tucking it underneath itself.

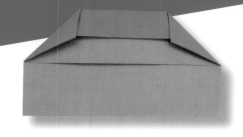

7 Repeat step 6 on the right-hand corner. The folds will be 'locked' in place by tucking them under and pressing.

8 Fold your paper vertically in half from right to left.

9 Fold the top flap to the right, making a new crease a short way from the central crease, but in the opposite direction.

10 Fold the right-hand edge of the wing over to the left to create a wing tip. It should only be a short way in, as shown.

11 Turn the plane over and repeat steps 9 and 10 to create the second wing and wing tip.

12 Adjust your wing tips and your Spade is ready to glide!

Upside-Down

Turn everything on its head with this craftily canny upside-down glider!

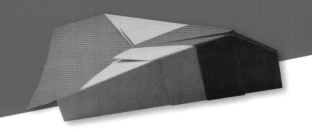

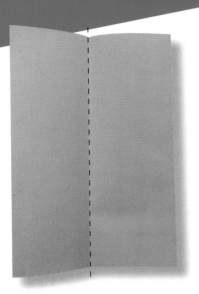

1 Place your paper so that it is portrait. Fold it from left to right down the centre line, then unfold it again.

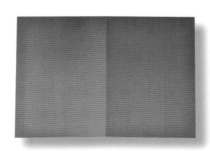

2 Now fold the paper in half again but horizontally from top to bottom.

3 Fold the top flap upwards to meet the top edge.

4 Now fold the new top edge downwards halfway, as shown. Your paper should now have three sections (or stripes) across its top half.

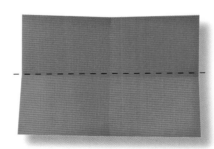

5 Turn your paper over and fold the bottom edge up to meet the top edge. Make a crease and unfold to reveal a cross where the two folds meet at the central point.

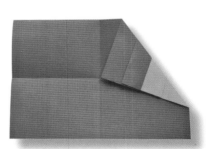

6 Now fold the top right-hand corner diagonally towards the centre point (where the cross is).

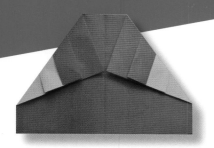

7 Repeat step 6 on the top left-hand corner, making sure the two corners meet at the centre cross point.

8 Fold your paper vertically in half from right to left.

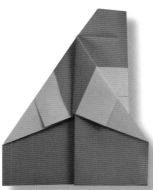

9 Now fold the top flap from left to right so that is parallel with the straight edge. This creates a wing.

10 Turn the plane over and repeat step 9 on the other side to create the second wing. Press firmly to create strong creases.

11 Open out the wings and you'll see the stripes across the top. Ready, steady, throw!

Pocket Glider

Air pockets are aplenty with this super-flying Pocket Glider.

1 Place your paper so that it is portrait. Fold it from left to right down the centre line, then unfold it again.

2 Now fold the paper in half from top to bottom, then unfold it. You have created a central cross where the creases meet.

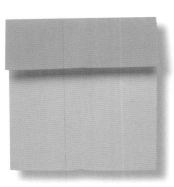

3 Fold the top edge of the paper downwards so the edge meets the central crease line that you created in step 2.

4 Now fold the top left-hand corner into the centre crease, making sure the edge aligns with if perfectly.

5 Repeat step 4 on the right-hand corner. Both corners should align along the centre crease.

6 Fold the top point downwards, stopping a short way from the bottom edge, as shown.

7 Now fold the bottom point upwards to align with the top straight edge of the paper. The point should fall directly in the centre crease.

8 Carefully fold in the top left-hand corner so that the top edge of your paper aligns with the centre crease. Unfold this.

9 Now, make another fold inwards so that the top edge of your paper aligns with the fold you created in step 8. Unfold this.

10 Repeat steps 8 and 9 on the top right-hand corner.

11 Finally, fold the top left-hand corner again but this time push the corner under the central pocket that has formed. It helps to pull this pocket outwards while you press the corner under. The remaining paper should fall diagonally from the centre of the pocket out towards the wing edge.

12 Repeat step 11 on the right-hand corner, then turn the plane over.

13 Press all your creases firmly and launch your glider by holding on to the pocket!

Awesome

This incredible gliding machine has magnificent folds for aerodynamic accuracy.

1 Place your paper so that it is landscape. Then fold it in half down the centre from left to right. Unfold it.

2 Now fold in the top left-hand corner towards the centre, making sure it aligns with the centre crease.

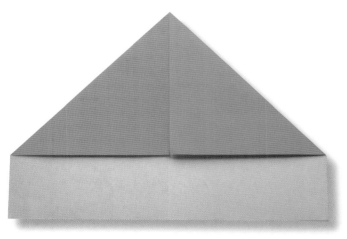

3 Repeat step 2 on the right-hand corner. Both corners should align at the centre crease.

4 Fold down the top point so it aligns with the bottom edge of the folds from steps 2 and 3.

5 Now fold down the top edge a short way, as shown.

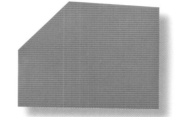

6 Fold your plane in half, from right to left, using the fold you made in step 1.

7 Make the first wing by folding the top flap back towards the right. Make the fold diagonally and press the crease firmly.

8 Turn the plane over and repeat step 7 to create the other wing. Make sure the second wing lines up with the first one.

9 Hold your glider by the central fold and watch it go! Awesome!

The Condor

This glider can swoop low and smoothly, just like a real condor!

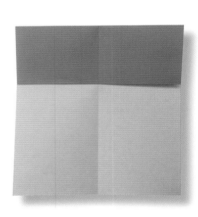

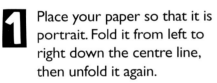

1 Place your paper so that it is portrait. Fold it from left to right down the centre line, then unfold it again.

2 Now fold the paper in half again, but this time horizontally from top to bottom. Unfold again.

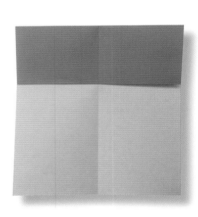

3 Fold down the top edge so it aligns with the horizontal centre crease.

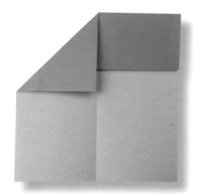

4 Fold the top left-hand corner inwards so that the top edge aligns with the centre crease.

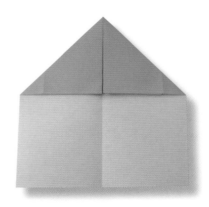

5 Repeat step 4 on the right-hand corner. Both corners should align along the central crease.

6 Fold the top point downwards using the fold you made in step 2 as your fold line.

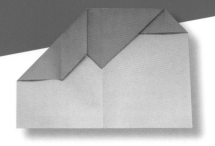

7 Now fold the top left corner inwards. It should run parallel to the centre crease, but be a short distance away, as shown.

8 Repeat step 7 on the top right corner. You will need to press the creases firmly as the paper becomes thicker.

9 Fold the plane in half vertically along the centre fold from left to right, using the fold you made in step 1.

10 Fold the top flap back over to the left to create the first wing. The fold should naturally sit where your fold from step 7 was made.

11 Now fold back the left edge a short way to create the wing tip, as shown.

12 Turn the plane over and repeat steps 10 and 11 to create the other wing and wing tip. Make sure your wing tips are the same size as each other.

13 Holding your plane by its central folds, open out the wings and adjust the wing tips – your glider is ready to take to the skies!

Arrows

Fast and direct, the Arrows are precision paper planes.

With arrows, it's all about the pointy nose. Control your plane's ability to climb or dive by angling the wing tips up or down.

Interceptor

The Interceptor is stealthy and manoeuvrable, so it's great for secret flights!

1 Place your paper so that it is portrait. Fold it from left to right down the centre line, then unfold it again.

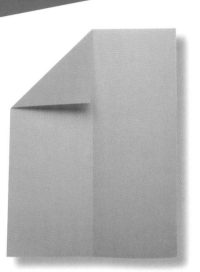

2 Fold the top left-hand corner down so that the top edge aligns with the centre crease.

3 Repeat step 2 for the top right-hand corner.

4 Now fold the left-hand side inwards so that the diagonal edge aligns with the centre crease.

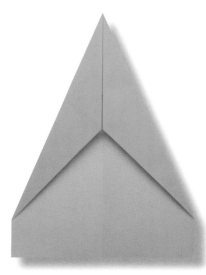

5 Repeat step 4 for the right-hand side. Make sure the edges align along the centre crease.

6 Now fold the paper downwards in half, so that the top point touches the bottom edge of the paper.

7 Fold the point back upwards, making a horizontal crease where the triangle meets the diagonal inner edges.

8 Turn your paper over and fold in half, vertically from right to left.

9 Now fold the bottom right corner up a little way, as shown.

10 Turn the paper over and repeat step 9 reversing the fold you just made.

11 Unfold the plane a little and push the lower triangle inwards. Then refold as before.

12 With the plane on its side, fold the top flap over to the right to create the first wing. The fold should be parallel to the main body of the plane.

13 Do the same with the other wing, so it aligns with the first.

14 Fold the bottom edge of the top wing upwards a short way, as shown.

15 Do the same with the other wing tip, making sure the folds align.

16 With its menacingly sharp nose and wing tips, your Interceptor is prepared for action!

Albatross

The Albatross is swift, strong and a super flyer.

1 Place your paper so it is portrait, then fold down the top left-hand corner to touch the right-hand edge. Unfold.

2 Repeat step 1 on the right-hand corner. This will create a cross shape on your paper.

3 Turn your paper over so that the cross shape created by the folds in steps 1 and 2 lifts slightly towards you.

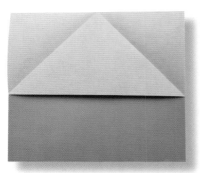

4 Now fold the top edge of the paper down horizontally, creasing at the central point of the cross shape. Unfold again.

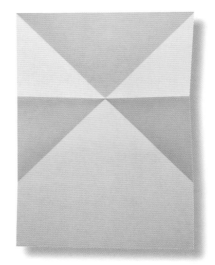

5 Turn your paper over again and fold it in half vertically from left to right. Unfold the paper again.

Arrows

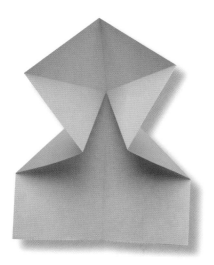

6 Carefully lift up the horizontal fold lines and push them together. Once they meet, a triangle will form on the top layer. Flatten this down.

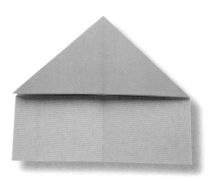

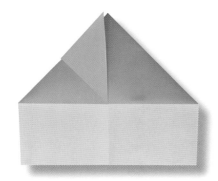

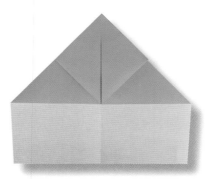

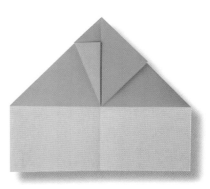

7 Fold the top left flap up to align with the centre crease.

8 Repeat step 7 on the top right flap.

9 Now fold the left-hand triangle upwards again so that it aligns with the centre crease.

49

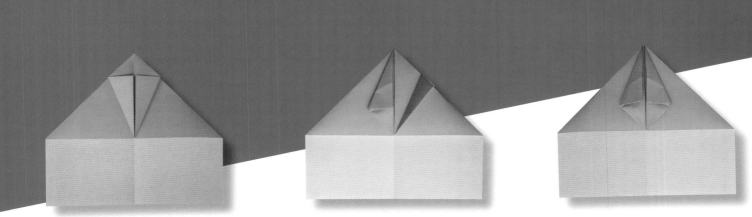

10 Repeat step 9 on the right-hand side. Then unfold both new folds.

11 Now, fold the left-hand triangle down so that it is aligned with the centre crease.

12 Repeat step 11 on the right-hand side. Unfold both new folds.

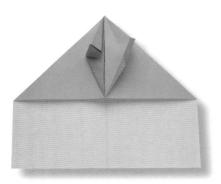

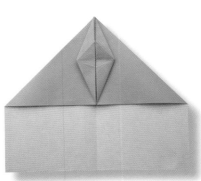

13 On the left-hand side, press down with your finger on the right and re-crease both diagonal folds. This should make the central section lift up. Pinch it with your fingers towards the centre crease to form a little raised triangle.

14 Repeat step 13 for the right-hand side, carefully pinching upwards the newly formed triangle shapes.

15 Press the pinched triangles upwards so they point towards the top of the paper.

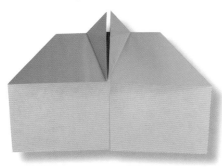

16 Now fold the top part of the paper backwards (away from you) horizontally, using the fold where the points of the central triangles are. This leaves the triangles sticking out at the top of the paper.

17 Now fold your paper in half vertically, from left to right.

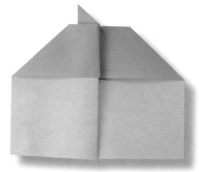

18 Fold the top flap over to the left to form one wing.

19 Turn the paper over and repeat step 18 to form the other wing.

20 Open out and make a small fold in the left wing to create the wing tip.

21 Repeat step 20 on the right-hand side to create the other wing tip. Your Albatross is fit for flight!

Barracuda

The Barracuda will cut through the air with its sharp nose!

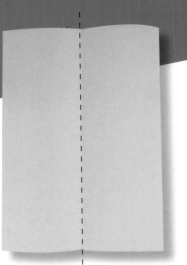

1 Place your paper so that it is portrait. Fold it from left to right down the centre line, then unfold it again.

2 Fold the top left-hand corner down so that the top edge aligns with the centre crease.

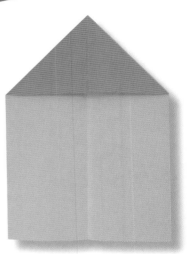

3 Repeat step 2 for the top right-hand corner. Leave these folds in place to create a triangle point at the top of the paper.

4 Now fold the top of the paper downwards diagonally. The right-hand side of the triangle should line up with the right-hand side of the paper. Unfold again.

5 Repeat step 4 on the other side, aligning the left-hand side of the triangle with the left-hand side of the paper. Unfold again.

6 Turn the paper over and you will see a cross-shape with the vertical fold running through it. Fold the top downwards horizontally, using the centre of the cross as a guide. Unfold again.

7 Turn the paper back over and you will see that the horizontal fold line lifts towards you. Pinch these together and refold the lower diagonal creases one at a time, beginning with the left. This will cause the paper to fold downwards so that the triangle points downwards.

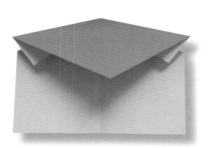

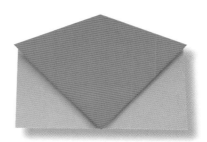

8 Now fold the point of the triangle back upwards, using the beginning of the diagonals as the guide for your horizontal crease.

9 Fold the left-hand side of the diagonal edge towards the right. Unfold.

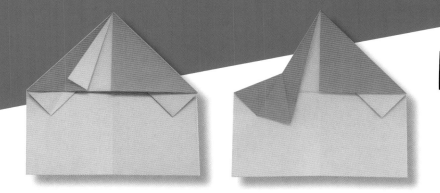

10 Now fold the left top flap a little way to the left. The edge should align with the crease from step 9. Repeat the fold you made in step 9 over the top of this smaller fold.

11 Repeat steps 9 and 10 for the right-hand side of the paper. The piece nearest to the centre fold will tuck underneath the bigger piece.

12 Tuck the bottom left point underneath itself, as shown.

13 Repeat step 12 on the right-hand side and press both sides down firmly.

14 Turn your plane over and fold vertically from right to left.

15 Fold the top flap over to the right, as shown. This creates the first wing.

16 Turn the plane over and repeat step 15 on the other side. Make sure the wings are symmetrical.

17 Creating wing tips for this plane is optional – if you want wing tips, fold back a narrow strip along each wing's edge.

18 Your Barracuda aircraft is ready for its first stealth mission!

Zip Zap

Watch this sharp arrow plane
zip-zap through the air!

1 Place your paper so that it is portrait. Fold it from left to right down the centre line, then unfold it again.

2 Fold the top left-hand corner inwards so the top edge aligns with the centre crease.

3 Repeat step 2 on the right-hand corner. Make sure both top edges align with the centre crease.

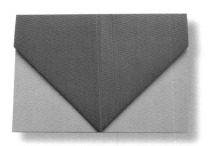

4 Fold the top point down so that it touches the bottom edge of the paper at the centre crease. Unfold again.

5 Now fold the top point downwards again so that it touches the centre point where the horizontal and vertical creases cross.

6 Fold the left-hand side of the paper diagonally upwards to the right. Use the left edge of the downward pointing triangle as your fold line. Unfold again.

7 Repeat step 6 for the right-hand side of the paper. You will see a cross shape as well as your horizontal and vertical fold lines.

8 Carefully lift up the horizontal fold lines and place them vertically down the centre of the paper. The top triangle will sit on top of them.

9 Fold your paper in half, vertically from right to left.

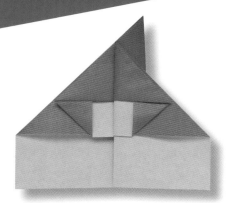

10 Now fold the left-hand side back to the right, a short way from the fold made in step 9, as shown.

11 Turn the plane over and repeat step 10 on the other side.

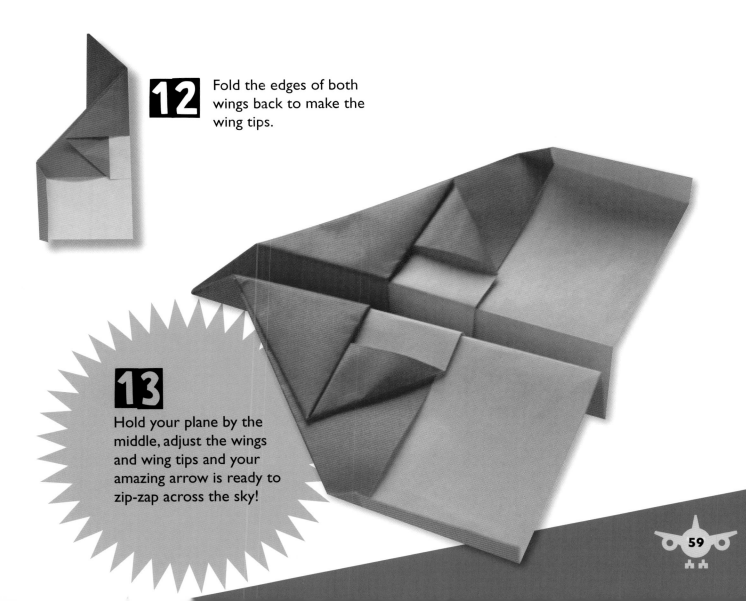

12 Fold the edges of both wings back to make the wing tips.

13

Hold your plane by the middle, adjust the wings and wing tips and your amazing arrow is ready to zip-zap across the sky!

Wings

They swoop, they soar: they are the wings!

Wing paper planes have large surface areas, making them very versatile indeed – they're also quick and easy to make. So go on, spread your wings and have a try!

Flying Wing

Create a plane with super-wide wings for indoor flying fun!

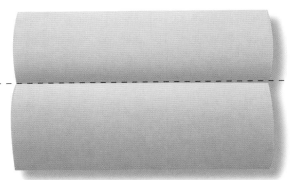

1 Place your paper so that it is landscape and fold it in half, horizontally from top to bottom. Unfold again.

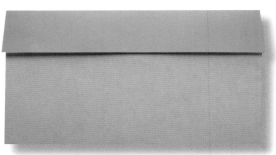

2 Fold the top down so that the top edge meets the centre crease.

3 Now fold the bottom edge upwards so that it stops a short way from the top edge, as shown.

4 Now fold down the top edge to overlap the paper you folded upwards in step 3.

5 Fold your paper in half, vertically from left to right.

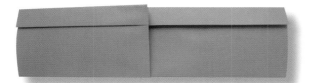

6 Fold back the top flap of paper from right to left, folding a short way in from the fold from step 5. This creates the first wing.

7 Turn the paper over and repeat step 6 to create the other wing.

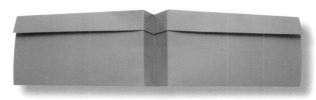

8 Open out the wings.

9 Fold back the wing edges to form wing tips and your super-wide Flying Wing plane is ready for take-off.

Kingfisher

Swoop and glide with this bird-like beauty of a paper plane.

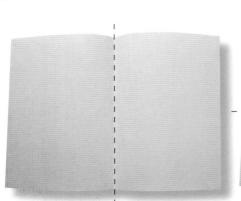

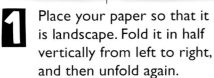

1 Place your paper so that it is landscape. Fold it in half vertically from left to right, and then unfold again.

2 Now fold the paper again, horizontally from top to bottom. Unfold again. The folds will have made a cross-shape.

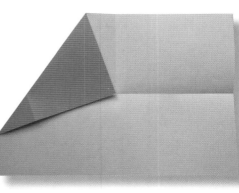

3 Fold the top left-hand corner down to meet the centre of the cross.

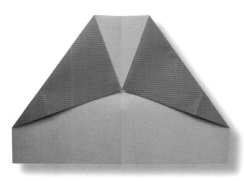

4 Repeat step 3 on the right-hand corner.

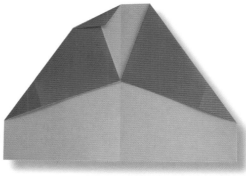

5 Now fold the new top left-hand corner downwards, diagonally so that the fold ends at the centre crease.

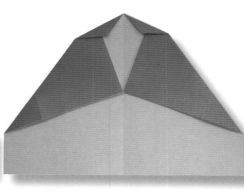

6 Repeat step 5 on the new top right-hand corner. Make sure the diagonal folds are symmetrical.

7 Fold the top point down so that it meets the bottom edge at the centre crease.

8 Now fold the bottom point upwards so that it falls a little way above the top edge of the paper.

9 Turn the plane over and fold in half, vertically from right to left.

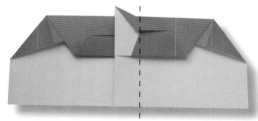

10 Fold the right edge back to the left to form the plane's body, then open out the wings, as shown. Fold the plane's body back over to the right, along the dotted line.

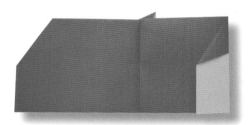

11 Turn over and fold the right edge of the first wing back towards the left, making the fold where the diagonal top edge begins. This creates the wing tip.

12 Do the same with the other wing tip, making sure both wing edges are aligned.

13 Spread your Kingfisher's wings and let it fly!

The Kite

Accurate and with massive wings; it can only be the Kite!

1 Place your paper so that it is portrait. Then, fold the top down, as shown.

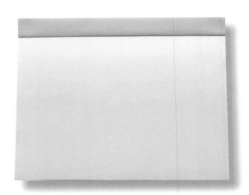

2 Repeat step 1 a total of eight times, each time folding the crease down firmly.

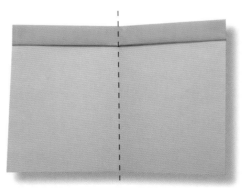

3 Now fold your paper in half, vertically from right to left.

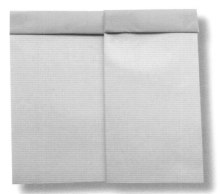

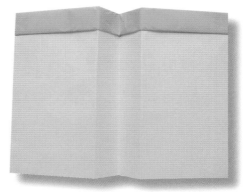

4 Fold back the right-hand side, making a crease a short way from the centre fold. This will create the first wing.

5 Turn the paper over and repeat step 4 to create the other wing. Make sure your wings align and their folds are symmetrical.

6 Your wing-whopper can take flight... up to the highest heights!

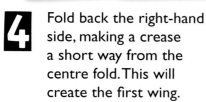

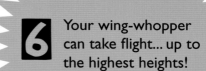

Glorious Glider

The Glorious Glider has angled wings and elegant wing tips.

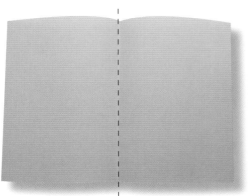

1 Place your paper so that it is landscape then fold it vertically in half from left to right. Unfold it.

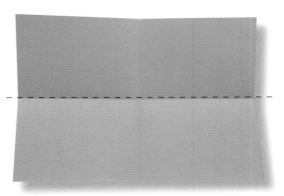

2 Now fold the paper in half, horizontally from top to bottom. Unfold again.

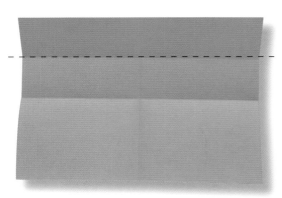

3 Fold the top edge downwards to meet the horizontal centre crease. Unfold again. You will have made two cross points.

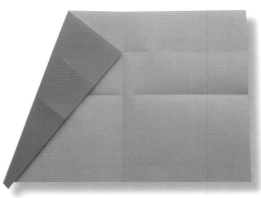

4 Fold the top left-hand corner inwards so the point meets the top cross.

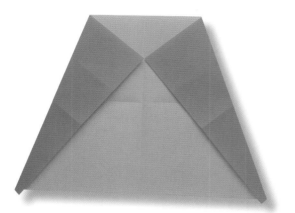

5 Repeat step 4 on the top right-hand corner so the two corners now meet at the centre crease.

6 Now fold the top edge downwards, using the top horizontal crease you made in step 3 as the fold line.

7 Fold the top edge downwards a short way, as shown. Press firmly as the paper becomes thicker.

8 Repeat step 7 twice so that the fold you created in step 6 is completely covered.

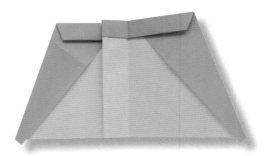

9 At the centre crease, fold the left side towards the right side, as shown, to make the plane's body.

10 Take the right-hand side of this new flap and fold it back over to the left a little way, as shown.

11 Now fold the right side over to the left side, making sure all the edges of your plane align. Press the folds firmly.

12 Your elegant glider can now fly high.

Manta-Ray

Intricate and exciting, give the Manta-Ray a go!

Wings

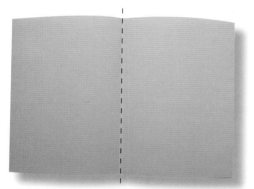

1 Place your paper so that it is landscape. Fold it in half, vertically from left to right. Unfold it.

2 Now fold the left-hand edge inwards to meet the centre crease. Unfold again.

3 Repeat step 2 on the right-hand side. Make sure the two edges align at the centre crease without overlapping. Unfold again.

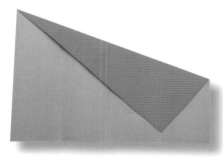

4 Fold the top right-hand corner downwards, making the crease from the top left-hand corner diagonally. The top right-hand corner should stop a short way from the bottom edge and align with the crease from step 3. Unfold again.

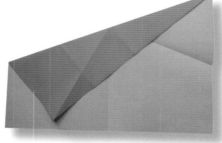

5 Repeat step 4 on the top left-hand corner. Make sure the corner aligns with the crease from step 2. Unfold again.

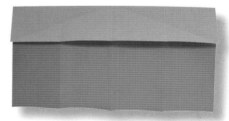

6 Turn the paper over and fold the top edge of the paper downwards. Use the cross point where the two diagonal folds meet the centre fold as the new fold line.

7 Turn the paper back over and the horizontal fold lines will lift up towards you. Lift these up and downwards, one at a time, and push flat.

8 When you have pushed both sides down, you will have a triangle shape at the top of the paper.

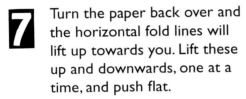

9 Fold the top left flap over to the right, opening out the previous fold you made.

10 Repeat step 9 on the top right-hand corner.

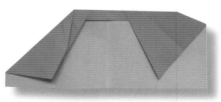

11 Turn the paper over and fold down the top point a short way, as shown. Make sure you align the point with the vertical centre crease.

12 Turn the paper back over and fold the left edge inwards using a previous fold line.

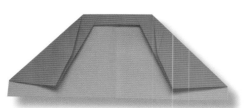

13 Repeat step 12 on the right-hand side.

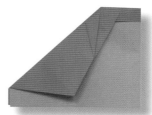

14 Turn the paper over again and fold it in half, vertically from right to left along the centre crease.

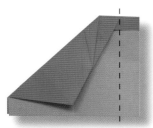

15 Fold the right-hand edge back a short way, where the dotted line is, to make the body.

16 Open out the wings, as shown, and fold the body back over to the right along the dotted line.

17 Your Manta-Ray is now ready to cut through the air.

And last but not least...

Why stick to ordinary aircraft when you can make these fantastical fliers with a difference? Let your imagination go wild with a paper UFO, a viper ring or the amazing shooting star!

The Remnant

Turn a spare part into a clever aircraft!

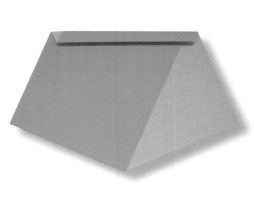

1 This plane can be made from any narrow rectangle of paper. Place it so that it is portrait.

2 Fold the top right-hand corner downwards to meet the bottom left-hand corner.

3 Turn your paper so that the bottom left-hand corner points downwards. Then, fold the top down a little, as shown.

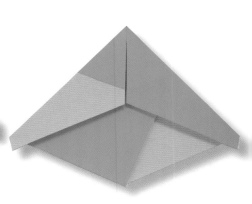

4 Fold the paper in half, vertically from left to right, then unfold.

5 Now fold the top right-hand corner downwards so the top edge aligns with the centre crease.

6 Repeat step 5 for the top left-hand corner.

8 Fold down the top point as shown. Press the crease firmly.

7 Turn the plane over so that both folds from steps 5 and 6 are facing away from you.

10 Fold the new left-hand edge back towards the right, making the crease a short way from the centre fold. This creates the first wing.

9 Now fold the plane in half, vertically from right to left. Make sure the edges align.

11 Turn the plane over and fold the right hand side over to the left, making the crease a short way from the centre fold.

12 Your Remnant may be small but it is perfectly formed – now see how far it can fly!

The Galleon

With back-to-front wings, this Galleon is a real futuristic flyer.

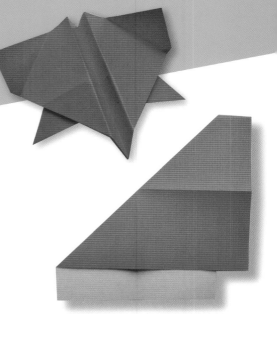

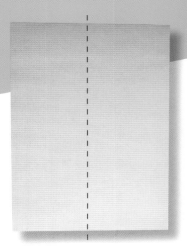

1 Place your paper so that it is portrait and fold it in half, vertically from left to right. Unfold.

2 Now fold the paper in half, horizontally from top to bottom. Unfold again.

3 Fold the top left-hand corner downwards diagonally. Make sure the horizontal fold line aligns with the vertical fold line. Unfold again.

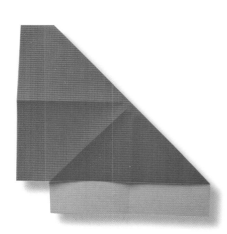

4 Repeat step 3 with the top right-hand corner. Make the crease in both directions along the diagonal fold line. Unfold again.

5 Turn the paper over and fold it in half, horizontally from top to bottom. This reverses the crease you made in step 2.

6 Turn the paper over again and the horizontal centre fold will lift towards you.

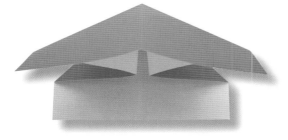

 Refold the lower diagonal folds on the left and then the right.

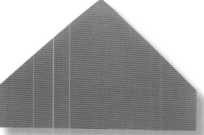

 You will now have a point at the top. Fold the point downwards so that it meets the centre crease at the bottom edge. Press firmly.

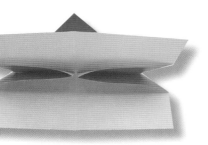

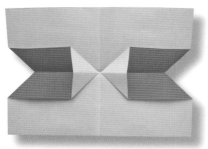

Turn the paper over and lift up the top layer of paper from the bottom edge. The paper will open up so you can squash down the two centre sections to make four new diagonal folds.

 Fold the new bottom edge upwards so it aligns as shown.

 Fold the left-hand corner of this narrow strip upwards so that the left edge aligns with the top edge.

12 Repeat step 11 on the bottom right-hand corner. Align in the same way.

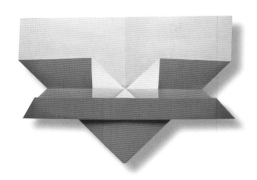

13 Now fold the bottom edge of the rectangular panel upwards and crease along the horizontal line.

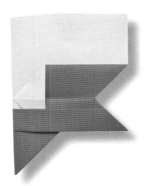

14 Turn the plane over so these folds are facing away from you, then fold it in half, vertically from right to left.

15 Fold back the top left-hand edge to create the first wing. Make the fold where the diagonal fold connecting the wing to the body occurs – a short way from the centre fold.

16 Turn the plane over and repeat step 14 to create the other wing. Make sure both wing edges align and do not overlap.

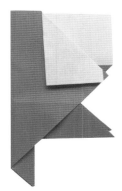

17 Create wing tips on both sides by folding the top corners towards the centre.

18 Adjust your wing tips and prepare to fly!

The Swallow

Narrow and swift, just like the bird –
see the Swallow swoop!

1
You will need a long, narrow rectangular piece of paper for this one. Place it so it is portrait.

2
Fold the top left-hand corner diagonally so that the top edge aligns with the right edge. Unfold.

3
Repeat step 2 on the top right-hand corner. Unfold and you'll see this has created a cross shape.

4
Turn the paper over and fold the top edge downwards, using the centre of the cross as your horizontal fold line. Unfold again.

5
Turn the paper over again and you will see that the paper lifts towards you along the horizontal centre fold. Pinch these towards you and refold the lower diagonal creases one at a time, starting with the left one.

6
As you press each diagonal fold, the top of the paper will naturally fold downwards, forming a triangle with a point at the top of the paper.

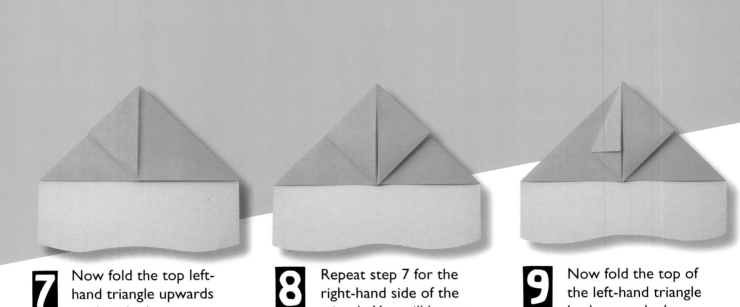

7 Now fold the top left-hand triangle upwards so that the bottom edge aligns with the centre fold.

8 Repeat step 7 for the right-hand side of the triangle. You will have a square shape on top of the triangle.

9 Now fold the top of the left-hand triangle back towards the centre fold. Then unfold.

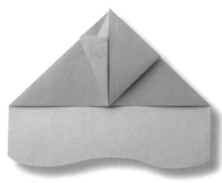
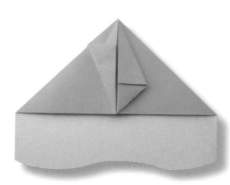

10 Fold up the bottom of the left-hand triangle, as shown.

11 Repeat step 9 on the right-hand side.

12 Repeat step 10 on the right-hand side. Then unfold both sides.

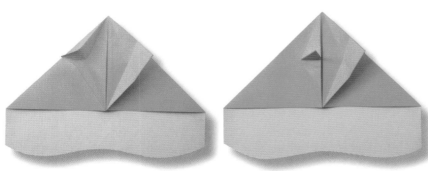

13 Holding down on the centre crease, pinch underneath the left-hand side of the square and push in towards the centre to form a point that sticks up off the paper.

14 Repeat step 13 for the right-hand side. You should now have a diamond shape at the centre of the paper with two points sticking up.

15

Now fold the left-hand side of the outer diagonal edge in towards the centre. Position it behind the central diamond shape.

16

Repeat step 15 on the right-hand side. Both diagonal edges should align along the centre fold, and be tucked behind the central diamond shape.

17

Turn the paper over so that all the folds are facing away from you. Now fold the top point downwards, making the fold line where the top of the diamond shape is.

18

Now fold the paper in half, vertically from right to left.

19

Fold the long left edge back to the right (to align with the central fold). This creates your first wing.

20

Repeat step 19 on the other side to create the other wing.

21

Open out the wings and your Swallow is ready to swoop!

Viper Ring

It's all in the throw with this unbelievable paper Viper Ring!

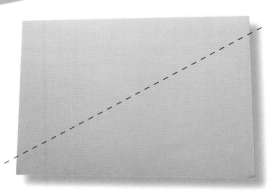

1 Place your paper so that it is landscape. Then, fold it diagonally, as shown. The fold should be a short way from the corners.

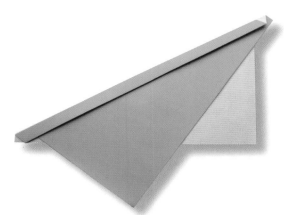

2 Fold the straight edge (where your first fold is) symmetrically inwards by about a finger width.

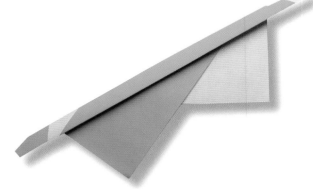

3 Repeat step 2 three times more to make this edge thicker. You should have four folds along the same long, narrow edge.

5 Using the folded edge, you will be able to join the two ends by inserting one into the other.

4 Now you need to carefully but firmly bend your paper round, keeping the long folded edge on the inside.

6 The four folds along the diagonal line will have created pockets at the edges in which you can find room to slot one side into the other to secure the ring shape.

7 It's a strange one for sure – throw it safely from a great height and watch it spin!

Helicopter

Drop this paper helicopter from a height to see it spin!

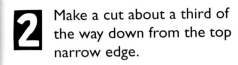

1 Take a long, narrow rectangle of paper and place it so that it is portrait.

2 Make a cut about a third of the way down from the top narrow edge.

3 Cut a little way into both of the longest edges, as shown. These cuts should be halfway down the paper and opposite each other.

4 Turn the paper over. Fold the bottom left-hand side in as far as the cut will allow. Repeat on the right-hand side. The flaps should overlap.

5 Fold the end of the long, narrow strip you have created in step 4 up a short way, as shown. This becomes the weight.

7 Stand safely in a high place to drop your Helicopter – watch it spin speedily to the ground! You may need to attach a paper clip for stability. Fold the rotors the other way to make it spin the opposite direction.

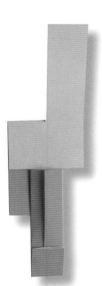

6 Now fold the top left flap backwards and then fold the top right flap down. These become the rotors.

Cross Dart

Aim far and high with this awesome paper dart plane!

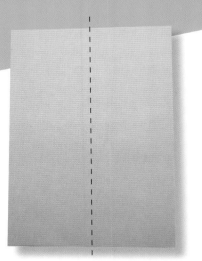

1 Place your paper so that it is portrait. Fold it in half vertically from left to right, then unfold.

2 Now fold the paper in half, horizontally from top to bottom. Unfold again. You will see a cross shape.

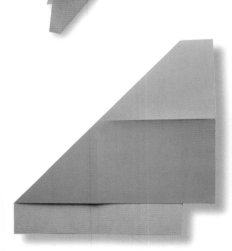

3 Fold the top left-hand corner down to the right, using the centre of the cross as a guide. The left-hand horizontal crease should align with the lower vertical fold. Unfold again.

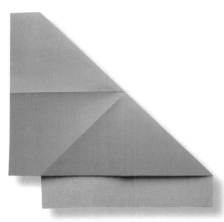

4 Repeat step 3 with the top right-hand corner. The right-hand horizontal crease should align with the lower vertical fold. Unfold and you will see a star shape.

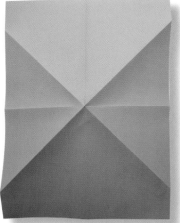

5 Turn the paper over, repeat the horizontal fold from step 2 and unfold again.

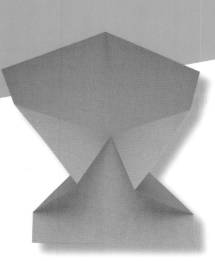

6 Turn the paper back over and you will see that the horizontal centre folds lift up towards you. Pinch these horizontal folds and, starting with the left side, fold downwards along the lower left diagonal crease.

7 Repeat step 6 for the right side, folding along the lower right diagonal crease. Press the top paper downwards so you have a triangle shape pointing away from you.

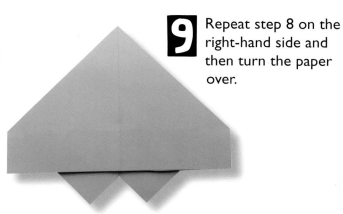

8 Now take the top part of the paper on the left-hand side and fold inwards so the diagonal edge aligns with the centre fold.

9 Repeat step 8 on the right-hand side and then turn the paper over.

10 Repeat step 8 on this side.

11 Repeat step 8 once more, on the right-hand side.

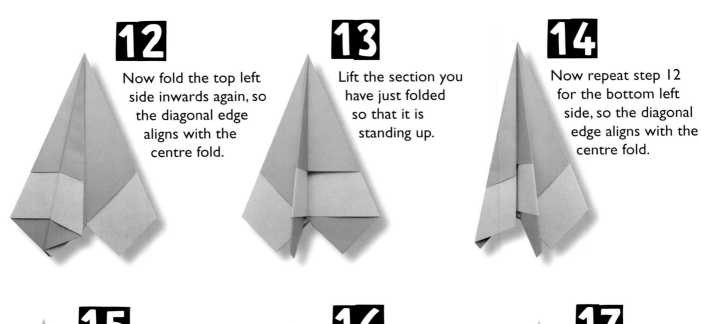

12
Now fold the top left side inwards again, so the diagonal edge aligns with the centre fold.

13
Lift the section you have just folded so that it is standing up.

14
Now repeat step 12 for the bottom left side, so the diagonal edge aligns with the centre fold.

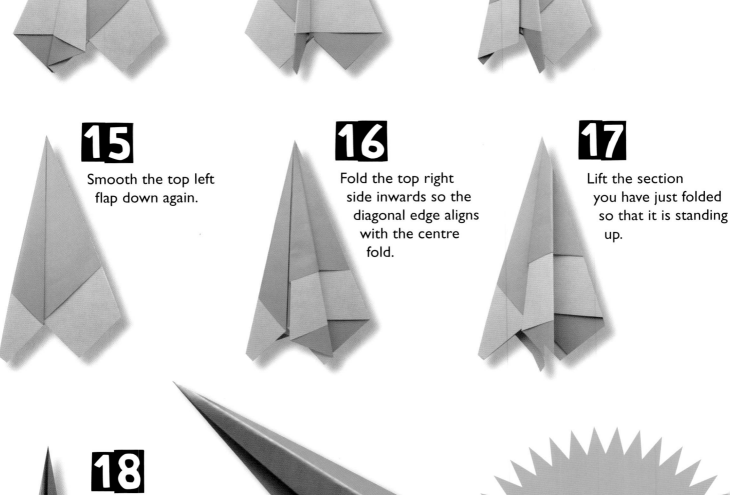

15
Smooth the top left flap down again.

16
Fold the top right side inwards so the diagonal edge aligns with the centre fold.

17
Lift the section you have just folded so that it is standing up.

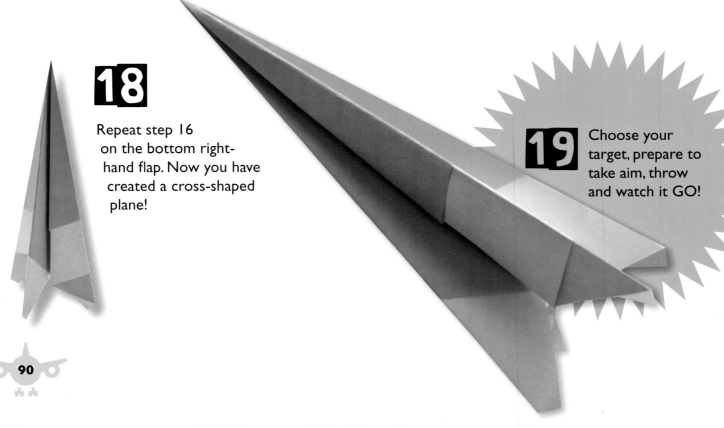

18
Repeat step 16 on the bottom right-hand flap. Now you have created a cross-shaped plane!

19
Choose your target, prepare to take aim, throw and watch it GO!

The UFO

Unidentified Flying Object last seen shooting through the air near you!

1 You need a large circle shape and there are several ways to make one: use a pencil and compass or draw around a circular object, e.g. a lid or reel of sticky tape. Carefully cut out your paper circle.

2 Fold the circle in half, vertically from left to right. Make sure the edges align so the fold is in the centre. Unfold.

3 Fold down the top edge a short way. Make sure the centre folds align. Unfold again.

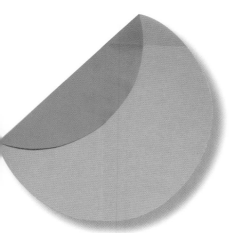

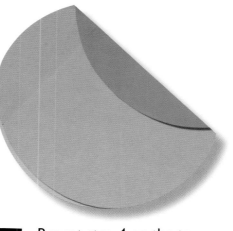

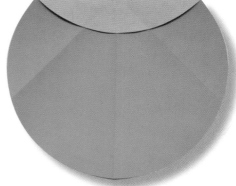

4 Now fold the top left edge, diagonally towards the centre. Align the left horizontal fold with the lower vertical fold.

5 Repeat step 4 on the top right edge, aligning the right horizontal fold with the lower vertical fold. Unfold to reveal a star shape.

6 Turn the paper over and make the horizontal fold again, using the fold line from step 3. Unfold again.

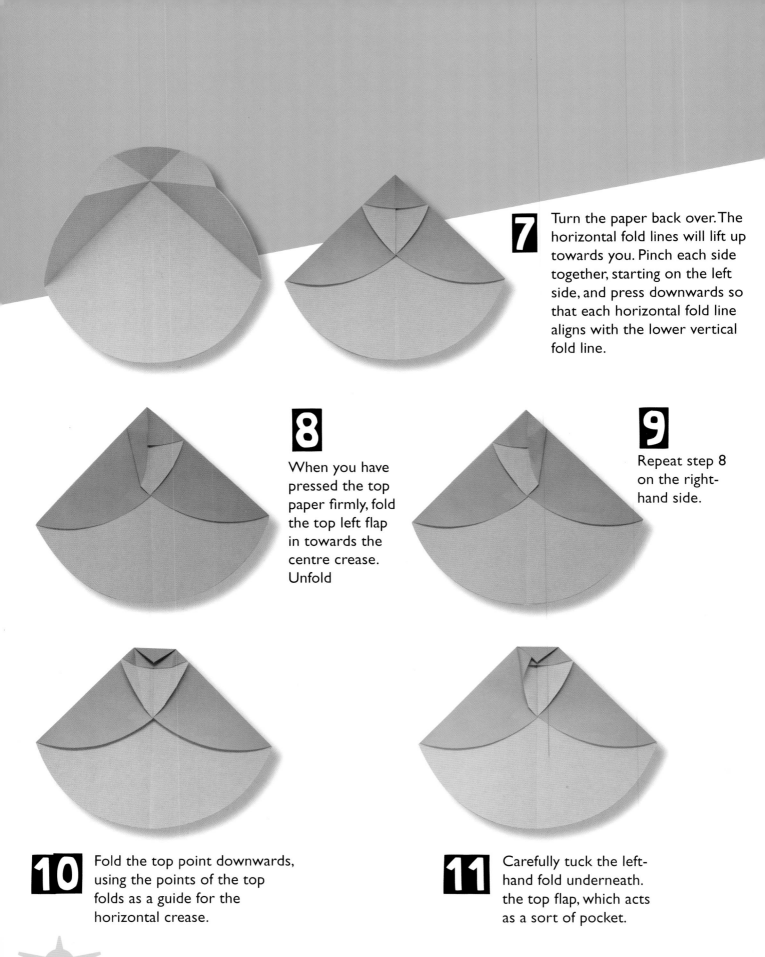

7 Turn the paper back over. The horizontal fold lines will lift up towards you. Pinch each side together, starting on the left side, and press downwards so that each horizontal fold line aligns with the lower vertical fold line.

8 When you have pressed the top paper firmly, fold the top left flap in towards the centre crease. Unfold

9 Repeat step 8 on the right-hand side.

10 Fold the top point downwards, using the points of the top folds as a guide for the horizontal crease.

11 Carefully tuck the left-hand fold underneath. the top flap, which acts as a sort of pocket.

12 Repeat step 11 on the right-hand side.

13 Turn the paper over so that the folded section is away from you. Fold the left diagonal edge inwards, aligning the crease with the top diagonal edge. This creates the first wing.

14 Repeat step 13 for the right side to create the other wing.

15 Turn the plane over so the wing tips face upwards. Your strange flying object is ready to take to the alien skies – we come in peace!

The Star

A flick of the wrist will shoot this star through the air!

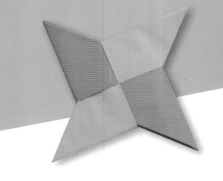

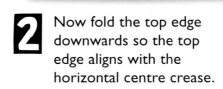

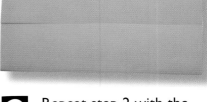

1 You will need two squares of paper for this Star. Fold the first in half, horizontally from top to bottom, then unfold.

2 Now fold the top edge downwards so the top edge aligns with the horizontal centre crease.

3 Repeat step 2 with the bottom edge, aligning the bottom edge with the centre crease.

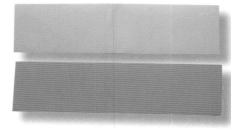

4 Fold the paper in half, horizontally from top to bottom.

5 Now fold the paper in half again, this time vertically from left to right. Unfold this crease.

6 Repeat steps 1 to 5 with the other piece of square paper. Ideally, choose a different colour.

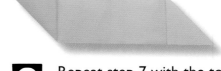

7 Take your first piece of paper and fold the bottom left-hand corner upwards so the left edge aligns with the top edge.

8 Repeat step 7 with the top right-hand corner, aligning the right edge with the bottom edge.

9 Take your second piece of paper and fold the top left-hand corner downwards so the left edge aligns with the bottom edge.

10 Repeat step 9 with the bottom right-hand corner, aligning the right edge with the top edge.

11 Take your first piece of paper and fold the top left edge diagonally to align with the centre crease.

12 Repeat step 11 with the bottom right edge. Align the bottom edge with the centre crease.

13 Take your second piece of paper and fold the bottom left edge diagonally to align with the centre crease. Repeat with the top right edge.

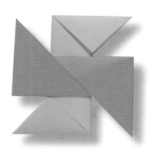

14 Turn the first piece of paper over and place it so the largest strip is vertical. Now place the second piece of paper across the first, horizontally.

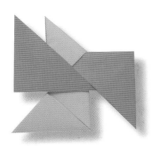

15 Now fold the top triangle (from the first piece of paper) downwards and tuck it into the left triangle (from the second piece of paper).

16 Fold the bottom triangle (from the first piece of paper) upwards and tuck it into the right triangle (from the second piece of paper). Press the folds firmly to make sure they are secure.

17 Carefully turn over the whole paper and fold the top right triangle (from the second piece of paper) diagonally and tuck it into the lower triangle (from the first piece of paper).

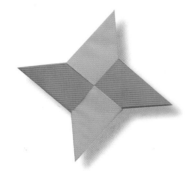

18 Fold the lower left triangle (from the second piece of paper) diagonally and tuck it into the upper triangle (from the first piece of paper).

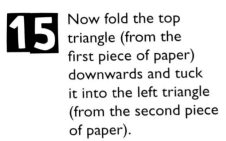

19 When you've pressed the creases down very firmly your amazing shooting star is ready to throw! Watch it go!